Original title:
The Quest for Life's Meaning (and More Coffee)

Copyright © 2025 Creative Arts Management OÜ
All rights reserved.

Author: Evelyn Hartman
ISBN HARDBACK: 978-1-80566-103-0
ISBN PAPERBACK: 978-1-80566-398-0

The Search in Every Aroma

In the cup of a morning brew,
Lies the wisdom we pursue.
Sipping gently, thoughts arise,
Dreams brewed hot with every size.

Pour it strong or make it weak,
Each slurp has a tale to speak.
Chasing answers in a swirl,
Coffee's charm makes thoughts unfurl.

Fable of the Java Seeker

Once a wanderer, mug in hand,
Sought the secrets of the land.
With each sip, a new delight,
Waking up the sleepy night.

His quest was steeped in caffeine flow,
Wherever he went, there was a show.
A splash of cream, a dash of fun,
Life's puzzle pieced with every run.

Navigating Shadows with Brewed Light

In the haze of the half-lit morn,
With a cup, all worries are shorn.
Through the fog, each sip I take,
Is a giggle shared with the wake.

When shadows loom, I laugh and sip,
Drowning doubts in a frothy dip.
Here's to finding joy anew,
In each drop, a brighter view.

Sips of Serenity

In the quiet of a cozy nook,
Lives the magic in the book.
Each chapter with a toasted roast,
Brews a smile I love the most.

With comfort in my warming hands,
I dream of far and distant lands.
Serenity in every mug,
Caffeinated hugs, oh what a tug!

The Elixir of Understanding

In a cup so warm and bright,
I ponder the meaning of day and night.
With each sip, a thought takes flight,
Is this brew my guiding light?

The barista smiles, oh what a tease,
As I sip through my existential freeze.
Maybe life's about beans and ease,
With a side of laughter and a sprinkle of cheese!

Mugfuls of Moments

A mugful of joy, I raise it high,
With each slosh and splash, I question why.
In this swirl of froth, I sigh,
Is happiness brewed, or just a lie?

Cream swirls like thoughts, a delightful mix,
With each sip, I play little tricks.
Dancing caffeine, oh what a fix,
Life's puzzles solved with a few quick licks!

Whispers Between Sips

Between sips, secrets pile,
Coffee whispers, makes me smile.
What's the point? Just stay awhile,
Let warmth wrap you, like a cozy file.

Stirring joy with sugar's kiss,
I ponder life, in a steamy bliss.
Each cup a puzzle, a warming quiz,
Who knew the key was a frothy fizz?

Roasted Ruminations

Dark roast wonders brewing near,
With every gulp, clarity is here.
By the bottom, it's all quite clear,
Perhaps life's sass is in the cheer!

Coffee grounds, my only guide,
In caffeine I trust, nowhere to hide.
With laughter's touch, and humor wide,
I sip my way through the cosmic ride!

Aroma of Aspiration

In morning's light, the coffee brews,
A fragrant promise, chase away the blues.
With every sip, I ponder deep,
What's life's true goal, or is it just sleep?

A mug in hand, I toast my dreams,
Espresso shots and frothy creams.
The world awakes, with laughter bright,
Let's caffeinate, and take flight!

From Beans to Beliefs

From humble beans, my faith does grow,
A daily ritual, as I sip slow.
Philosophers ponder, while I just sip,
Is enlightenment found in each little drip?

Dark roast thoughts, so rich and bold,
Do I find wisdom, or just clichés told?
With every pour, my mind starts to spin,
Just pass the cream, let the day begin!

Caffeine Conversations

Around the table, we share our plans,
Steaming cups in our eager hands.
"Life is short," one starts to say,
"Let's drink this brew and seize the day!"

Sip and giggle, the ideas flow,
In coffee's warmth, we steal the show.
With each loud laugh, we gain more zest,
Is this our journey? I'd call it best!

Brewed Reflections

Steam clouds rise like thoughts unspooling,
As I sip slowly, my mind is cooling.
Reflection's brew in my favorite mug,
Do I seek meaning, or just a hug?

Each sip's a quest, rich and profound,
In the java jigsaw, what's yet to be found?
With frothy art and quirky foam,
I raise my cup—a heart feels home!

Caffeine Dreams

In the midnight hour, I sip with glee,
Brewed elixirs dance wild and free.
What is the secret, oh potion bold?
A journey untold, a mystery to unfold.

Espresso shots make me think real deep,
What's life's meaning? Oh, just let me sleep!
I brainstorm with froth on my upper lip,
As thoughts swirl round like a caffeinated trip.

Beans of Insight

The coffee beans whisper, secrets shared,
As I ponder the universe, thoughts laid bare.
Arabica or Robusta? Such choices abound,
Sipping reflections, where answers are found.

With each little cup, my worries disperse,
Finding the meaning, or maybe a verse.
In this bittersweet brew, life makes a claim,
Do I seek wisdom, or just play the game?

Journey Through a Java Landscape

Across the land of mugs and steam,
I wander with purpose, or so it would seem.
The road is paved with ground-up beans,
Sipping my way through caffeine-filled dreams.

In this java landscape, all paths converge,
As dainty sips lead to a caffeine surge.
I laugh at the chaos, I dance with the grind,
In the quest for answers, they're just behind.

Stirring Thoughts

A spoon in my cup, I circle and swirl,
In deep contemplation as the coffee unfurl.
What to make of this life, bold and sweet?
Maybe it's better with a muffin to eat.

With a dash of sugar and cream on the top,
I ponder existence, then suddenly stop.
Life's not just riddles, it's just like this brew,
A splash of the silly, a hint of the true.

The Flavor of Purpose

In a cup of joy, I seek delight,
A splash of dreams, both day and night.
Stirring thoughts in warm embrace,
Finding purpose in this caffeinated space.

With every sip, a quest unfolds,
Stories brewed, both new and old.
The beans whisper secrets to the wise,
Life's flavor hidden in a warm surprise.

Brews of Belief

In mugs of magic, faith takes flight,
Each brew a spark on a sleepy night.
Frothy dreams topped with whipped cream cheer,
Beliefs ignited, there's nothing to fear.

Pour it strong, this blend divine,
In each sip, feel the stars align.
From press to drip, the tales will flow,
With every gulp, adventure grows.

Aroma of Hope

A whiff of warmth, it fills the air,
With hopes steeped bold, beyond compare.
Brewing dreams in my tiny pot,
Mmm, those hopes are brewed quite hot!

With laughter served alongside my cup,
I rise above when spirits sup.
In pitter-patter of rain or sun,
The aroma blends, life's just begun!

Uncharted Flavors

Embarking on sips of the unknown,
Chasing whims with a coffee cone.
From mocha mischief to chai delight,
Each taste reveals a new insight.

Life's menu, vast, with quirky blends,
Who knew flavors could be such friends?
So here's a toast to what's in store,
In this swirling cup, let's brew some more!

The Elixir of Insight

In a cup, the world does swirl,
Thoughts like bubbles, start to twirl.
A sip of dark, the mind's delight,
Philosophy brewed, just feels so right.

Mysteries rise with every pour,
Life's questions dance, I want for more.
In caffeine's grip, the answers gleam,
Or maybe just a drowsy dream.

Grounds for Exploration

With grounds in hand, I boldly dare,
To ponder life, and maybe stare.
Each little bean, a tale unfolds,
Of laughter, love, and coffee molds.

Around the mug, ideas flow,
What's deep in thought, we want to know.
To sip and think from dawn till night,
In caffeinated bliss, our spirits light.

Refilling the Soul

A steaming cup, my trusted friend,
I lift you high, my daily trend.
With every sip, the heart takes flight,
In joy and caffeine, the soul feels right.

Oh, fill me up, don't let it stop,
To search for meaning, I shall hop.
In every drop, a thought anew,
Is life about the coffee brew?

Coffee and Contemplation

A latte swirl, a frothy cap,
I sit and think, perhaps a nap.
The world outside moves fast, it seems,
But here I pause, in coffee dreams.

With every sip, I ponder wide,
What makes me happy, what's inside?
A jolt, a laugh, a playful tease,
Could meaning lie within the trees?

Searching for Purpose in Each Drop

In the morning light, I rise,
Hoping coffee clears my eyes.
A sip, a hope, a little cheer,
What's the point? I'm still not clear.

From beans to grind, it's quite a ride,
With each warm cup, my dreams collide.
To find the answers, oh so deep,
Or just the caffeine boost I seek!

With frothy foam and cream delight,
I ponder life, it feels so right.
But wait, is that a bitter taste?
Perhaps I need more coffee, haste!

So let's brew on, forget the strife,
In mugs, we find that spark of life.
With laughter bubbles, joy can sprout,
In every drop, I live without doubt.

Brews of Existence

Life's a blend of joy and woes,
Like coffee grounds and water flows.
Stirred with sugar, oh so sweet,
I ponder if I'm on my feet.

A double shot, a heavy sigh,
What am I doing? Oh, just why?
The universe in every cup,
I sip and wonder, will I erupt?

The perks of coffee cloud my mind,
In every brew, new thoughts I find.
But with each slurp, it seems unclear,
Is this the truth, or just my beer?

Let's grind it out, sip through the day,
In mugs of dreams, we find our way.
With every laugh and hearty glow,
I'm brewing life, just take it slow.

Coffee-Stained Reflections

With splashes brown on every page,
I scribble thoughts, feel quite the sage.
Each cup spills dreams and silly schemes,
In porcelain vessels, life redeems.

Reflections dance in steaming brew,
Decaf or bold—what's right for you?
I ponder deep, yet giggle too,
Why can't espresso solve my boo-hoo?

Late nights spent in darkened cafes,
Chasing answers in caffeine haze.
Life's meaning masked in latte art,
Where froth meets soul, the fun can start.

So here I sit, with coffee stains,
A canvas filled with joyful gains.
With every sip, a grin so wide,
Life's quirks blend well, let's take that ride!

Sip and Seek: A Journey Within

With every sip, I seek and strive,
To find the magic that's alive.
In every mug, a story waits,
Like sips of dreams on different plates.

I travel far with every brew,
Through wild ideas and scents so new.
A splash of fun, a dash of zest,
In coffee's grip, I feel so blessed.

A quirky quest, a joyful mess,
I chase the truth, I must confess.
But is it here, or just a joke?
In laughter's warmth, my soul awoke.

So let's keep pouring, make a splash,
In life's great dance, let's lose the bash.
With cups raised high, we'll find the way,
In playful sips, we seize the day.

Wakeful Wanderings

In a world of dreams I roam,
Searching far from my home.
With a mug in my hand, I'm bold,
Finding meaning in sips, uncontrolled.

The sun peeks through, my eyes do squint,
Philosophers ponder, my brain takes a hint.
A caffeine kick, my brain's best friend,
On this journey, may my mug never end.

Thoughts float by like clouds in the sky,
As I sip and gaze, letting worries fly.
Do ducks need coffee? I ponder aloud,
While the barista grins, serving the crowd.

With each gulp, I feel so bright,
The world's a jest, oh what a sight!
Finding wisdom with each brew,
And maybe a donut or two.

Steam and Solitude

In a café nook, I sit with cheer,
Embracing silence, or maybe a leer.
The steam from cups dances and twirls,
While I scribble notes on napkins and swirls.

Each sip's a question, bold and clear,
Why do I laugh? Is it just the cheer?
Philosophy slips into my cup,
As I stir my thoughts and drink it up.

A pastry's allure might cause a pause,
Yet the steaming brew earns my applause.
Is life a whirl of grind and brew?
Or just an espresso shot, too good to be true?

With every laugh, I ponder the chase,
For funny sentiments in this daily race.
Meeting meaning in the froth on top,
And the heartwarming vibe that makes me stop.

The Aroma of Discovery

The morning sun, a golden hue,
Brewing thoughts with a hint of dew.
What is this life, I muse with a grin,
Is the secret hidden in latte skin?

Beneath the foam, some wisdom brews,
With every sip, I share my views.
Do beans hold secrets of what is right?
Or just keep me buzzing from morning to night?

As I ponder, laughter weaves through air,
A spoonful of cream, oh buddy, beware!
I uncover mysteries in every cup,
And maybe, just maybe, a hiccup or sup.

Finding life's purpose in the marbled designs,
Lost in thought, the coffee entwines.
So here's to the sips, the laughs, the climb,
For I jest with my cup, not caring for time.

Brewed Awakening

In a java jungle, I stake my claim,
Hunting for meaning, what a wild game!
With mugs in hand, we embark with zest,
Chasing answers in a caffeine quest.

Is existential dread just a burnt roast?\nOr is it life's way of giving a boast?
I giggle at cat videos on my screen,
While the barista yells, "Another caffeine!"

With each delicious, steamy drop,
Thoughts bubble up, I can't make them stop.
What's the meaning of life? I cry in glee,
It might just be donuts and extra coffee!

So let's laugh and sip, enjoy every taste,
Finding joy in this crazy, wild race.
For with each little sip, my worries flee,
Awake to the fun of absurdity.

Exploration in Every Pour

In a cup of brew, the world unfolds,
Dreams steep longer, as the caffeine molds.
Sips like laughter, it's warm and bright,
With each little gulp, I take my flight.

Mismatched mugs and sugar spills,
Mapping out time with frothy thrills.
A coffee map, each drop a clue,
Brewing up truths I never knew.

A stroll to the kitchen, my trusty guide,
In the land of beans, I take great pride.
Pondering life, what should I do?
Should I get cream, or just stick with brew?

Espresso shots, wisdom in disguise,
Unraveling puzzles with sleepy eyes.
A jolt of fun in every sip,
Maybe the secret's in the perfect trip.

The Last Drop of Wonder

In the bottom of the cup, I find,
A philosopher's thoughts, brewed and blind.
Stirring chaos with sugar and cream,
Chasing answers like a coffee dream.

Each sip a giggle, or maybe a sigh,
With caffeine-induced clarity, oh my!
I ponder the universe while I sip,
Searching for truth in this foamy trip.

Brewing Introspection

Morning rituals with beans and grind,
Seek meaning in the steam, unwind.
A splash of milk, a sprinkle of fate,
Whisking through thoughts, I contemplate.

My cup overflows with thoughts both bright,
Will I solve life's riddles by morning light?
With every gulp, I twist and twirl,
In this brewing chaos, my mind's in a whirl.

The Sip of Existence

A little sip, a chance to pause,
Wondering if life has any laws.
Is it brewed strong or weakly poured?
I drift into thought, feeling adored.

The last swig's bitter, a truth unfolds,
With frothy truths, my spirit holds.
Do beans have secrets? Oh, what a ride,
In this caffeinated chaos, I take pride.

Pouring Over Life's Questions

Pouring thoughts like coffee, rich and hot,
Should I chase dreams or settle for what I've got?
The kettle sings of wisdom's brew,
Each drop revealing something new.

As I slurp and ponder, I start to see,
Life drips slowly, like caffeine's decree.
With each playful sip, I mock and jest,
This mug's a mystery that won't let me rest.

Sipping on Serenity

In my cup, a world resides,
Each sip, a joy that collides.
Stirring dreams with cream on top,
Finding peace, I will not stop.

Brewed adventures in a pot,
Seeking meaning, maybe not.
A splash of sugar, laughter bright,
Life's mysteries brewed just right.

Beans and Beyond

Dark and rich, the aroma calls,
Fueling laughs in cafe halls.
Out of this mug, wisdom flows,
As I sip, my spirit grows.

With every grind, a thought appears,
Do I ponder life or just my fears?
Take a sip, and let it slide,
Each tiny bean a hopeful guide.

Awakening in Every Mug

Morning comes, with sleepy eyes,
But that brew, oh what a surprise!
Steaming cups of liquid cheer,
Perk me up; let's persevere.

Velvet swirls, a frothy dance,
Life's puzzle needs a second glance.
With caffeine dreams, I take a ride,
Curious joy, my faithful guide.

Creating Meaning One Brew at a Time

Each brew brings whispers of delight,
In the steam, I find my flight.
Mugs unite us, laugh and share,
New adventures brew in the air.

Philosophizing, sip by sip,
In my cup, my logic dips.
Anchored thoughts in frothy waves,
Meaning brewing, oh how it saves.

Sips of Serendipity

In the morning sun, my mug does shine,
Coffee swirls, a dance divine.
I ponder if my toast will pop,
While dreams of grandeur start to drop.

Steam rises up like little dreams,
I sip on hope, or so it seems.
Life's answers brewed with a sprinkle of cream,
Can caffeine fuel a better scheme?

Sometimes I spill, a liquid mess,
As I muse on life's great quest.
Do socks have pairs, or lose their way?
In caffeine dreams, they dance and sway.

With every sip, a laugh and cheer,
Finding joy in cups of beer.
A paradox upon my desk,
Are drinks of joy a simple jest?

Reflections in a Coffee Cup

In the depths of my coffee cup,
I find my thoughts and hiccups sup.
What is life, I sip and think,
While floating crumbs begin to sink.

A splash of milk clears my view,
Like revelations that feel so new.
Should I reflect or should I nap?
In caffeinated dreams, I'll take a lap.

The world turns bright with every pour,
But spills remind me not to bore.
Do sugar cubes hold the secret key?
To life's great truths or just sweet tea?

In every sip, I find a joke,
Between the lines, my thoughts provoke.
Life's mysteries bubble and churn,
As I wait for more beans to learn.

Echoes of Purpose

With every cup, I ponder fate,
What's my path? Should I just wait?
The coffee brews, and so do plans,
Riding waves of caffeine fans.

A spoon stirs chaos in my mind,
Do I seek joy or simply grind?
Life's puzzles dance like shadows cast,
In coffee's warmth, I sip and fast.

I contemplate the watchdog's bark,
Is purpose found or just a lark?
A sip of dark and a dash of spice,
Life's complexities served up nice.

But laughter bubbles with each drop,
In frothy cups, the worries stop.
The quest for answers fuels the grind,
In every cup, life's joys aligned.

Mornings of Contemplation

In morning light, I take a seat,
With coffee warm, my day's offbeat.
I wonder if my breakfast sings,
As caffeine dreams unravel wings.

With every gulp, new thoughts align,
Is this the day I truly shine?
Or should I nap through all the noise,
And sip on thoughts of simpler joys?

The clock ticks on, a steady dance,
While I hold hope like a chance romance.
When life gets rough, I brew some more,
In coffee's embrace, my spirit soars.

So here's to mornings, bright and bold,
To cups of coffee, and tales retold.
In every sip, a giggle thrives,
As I toast to good and caffeinated lives.

Pouring Out Soul

In a mug so warm, dreams collide,
Coffee fills gaps, where thoughts might hide.
Stirring my spirit, a dance in the brew,
Finding lost laughs in a latte or two.

With every sip, I ponder and sip,
This java's my guru, it's quite the trip.
Balancing beans with a dash of fun,
Life's deep mysteries? Let's brew another one.

Reflections in Dark Roast

In the dark roast depths, I search for cheer,
Life's little puzzles hide in here.
A swirl of cream, philosophic delight,
Who knew my mug had insights so bright?

Sipping slowly, the clock ticks away,
Wearing my wisdom like a frothy bouquet.
Each thought percolates, rich and divine,
Do I need a philosopher or just more wine?

Steps Through Grounded Thoughts

With every step, my beans I crunch,
Philosophy brews with each morning brunch.
Is it the filter, or maybe the grind,
That fuels the questions echoing in my mind?

Strolling the aisles of my caffeinated dreams,
Each bag of coffee bursts at the seams.
From espresso to drip, bold flavors impart,
It's a journey for reason, captured in art.

A Journey with Every Grind

As I grind the beans, a quest begins,
Each turn of the wheel brings potential wins.
Will it be light, dark, or something anew?
My hopes bubble up in this caffeinated brew.

Navigating life with a cup in hand,
Frothing thoughts like a bold marching band.
In this warm cocoon, I find my way,
Cheers to the chaos of another great day!

The Journey of Every Sip

In the café, I ponder wise,
What's the secret in the skies?
Is it in the brew I sip?
Or just caffeine's fleeting grip?

With each cup a riddle unfolds,
Stories of adventures bold.
Should I add milk, or just go black?
Will this choice keep me on track?

I chase dreams in a porcelain maze,
Finding joy in daily craze.
Each gulp brings a chuckle or two,
As I sip my way to the truth.

So here's to the steaming mug,
That gives my soul a warm hug.
Life's questions swirl in mystery,
Brewed strong, it's a comedy!

Searching for Essence

With a cup in hand, I initiate,
A quest beyond the kitchen plate.
What defines this curious hunt?
Is it espresso or just a stunt?

Beans and brews in endless chase,
A flavor burst, a warm embrace.
But do I sip for truth or cheer?
Or just to stay awake all year?

Barista smiles with playful quirk,
Do I need wisdom in my perk?
Or is it laughter I pursue,
As coffee drips, and life feels new?

Dancing mugs in the morning light,
They hold my dreams, they feel just right.
In every drop, a jest or two,
Searching for essence, I find humor too!

Mugs and Mysteries

Mugs line up with stories bold,
Each sip a chapter to be told.
With a dash of sugar, a splash of cream,
Am I awake, or lost in a dream?

From dark roast depths to frothy peaks,
Life's greatest secrets are what each seeks.
Does the answer linger at the bottom?
Or is it somewhere I forgot 'em?

Caffeine high, I stretch my mind,
Finding joy in things designed.
With laughter bubbling, I sip profound,
In every mug, new friendships found!

So let's toast to mugs and mystery,
In this play of life, there's history.
Raise a cup to let humor reign,
With each refill, forget the mundane!

Tasting the Infinite

In a world where beans collide,
I embark on a brew-filled ride.
Taste the bitter, savor the sweet,
While the universe stirs at my feet.

Pouring dreams into the cup,
Hoping that all will bubble up.
With each slurp, I ponder deep,
Questions that tickle, thoughts that leap.

Is wisdom found in a caramel swirl?
Or do I just need life's coffee pearl?
In the java jigsaw, I take my seat,
Finding absurdity in every beat.

So let's sip on this cosmic brew,
With laughter echoing, deep and true.
Each cup tells jokes of time and space,
Tasting the infinite, life's funny chase!

Awakened by Aroma

In the morning light, I rise with glee,
The scent of coffee calls out to me.
I stumble to the pot, a sleepy parade,
My dreams drift away, as hot liquid's made.

Cream and sugar, my daily brew,
I ponder the universe and its cosmic hue.
As I sip, I reflect on life's vast plan,
Who knew that beans could help a man?

With every gulp, enlightenment calls,
Philosophy pours as the coffee falls.
I laugh at the thought—so quirky, so bright,
Found clues to existence in each joyful bite.

So I sit and ponder, mug held tight,
In this caffeinated bliss, I find delight.
Life's riddles unravel with each joyful sip,
Awakened by aroma, I grasp at the quip.

Journey from Bean to Being

Oh, coffee bean, your journey's grand,
From distant fields to my waiting hand.
Crushed and brewed, you whisper low,
Secrets of life in each scrumptious flow.

A dance with the grinder, a whirl and a spin,
The morning routine begins with a grin.
As steam rises up, my worries retreat,
A sip of pure joy, oh, life's bittersweet.

With each jolt, I philosophize,
Are we just beans in a world full of skies?
Or is it the grind that shapes us anew,
Like filters that strain the dreams we pursue?

Through laughter and froth, I toast to the day,
In quest for good brew, I find my own way.
So cheers to the wanderers, both near and far,
Our mugs raised high, beneath the same star.

Awakening Shadows

My dear cup of joy, in shadows I dwell,
With each sip of warmth, I break life's spell.
The darkness recedes, the caffeine ignites,
And suddenly, all of my worries take flight.

I ponder the essence of midnight and noon,
As I sip my elixir, I'll hum a tune.
With each drop of magic, absurd thoughts arise,
Who knew existentialism lived in disguise?

From dusk to the dawn, the grind keeps me sane,
Chasing my thoughts on a sugar-filled train.
The brew sparks my musings, absurd and profound,
While pondering why socks so often get found.

In the realm of the beans, I giggle and sigh,
As life spins around like a caffeinated pie.
With laughter abounding in my cozy lair,
In shadows awoken, I float on a dare.

Brews of Existence

In the depths of my mug, I find life's deep truth,
A dance of the beans from my youth to uncouth.
The bubbles arise, like ideas in flight,
Brews of existence keep the world bright.

I question the cosmos with every small sip,
Thinking maybe my cat is a galactic trip.
A playful concoction of froth and of dreams,
In coffee's embrace, nothing's quite as it seems.

So I laugh at the chaos as I pour my own fate,
Swirling around like a latte on a plate.
A philosopher's drink in a cup made of clay,
Each slurp leads to wonder, come what may.

From the kitchen to the stars, on this caffeinated road,
I gather the laughter, share each little ode.
So let's lift our mugs to the highs and the lows,
In brews of existence, life joyful, it flows.

Grains of Understanding

In the cup, a world awaits,
Filled with dreams and coffee fates.
Each sip a journey, bold and bright,
Searching for truth in the morning light.

Stirring thoughts with every swirl,
As caffeine makes the mind unfurl.
Why do we ponder, why do we sigh?
Are we just beans in the sky?

Pour it hot, let it flow,
Glimpses of wisdom start to show.
Between sips and savories,
Life's riddles danced, like swaying trees.

A latte foams with artful grace,
Life's conundrums in a warm embrace.
Maybe the meaning's in the brew,
Or just the way it warms me too.

Whispers of Espresso

A shot of dark, a rush of glee,
Whispers of truths in mystery.
Beneath a froth, the tales unfold,
Of moments shared, and hearts of gold.

What do I seek in this tiny cup?
A universe, a hopeful sup.
Each espresso a quirky thought,
Life's grand answers with every shot.

Steam rising high like dreams at play,
Searching for meaning in this ballet.
Every drop's a spark of jest,
Life's absurdities, simply zest!

Amidst the clatter, coffee spills,
In search of wisdom, caffeine thrills.
So here's to the beans, eternally bold,
With laughter found in stories told.

Revelations with Every Roast

As coffee brews, I come alive,
In the aroma, thoughts derive.
Roasting deep, like minds put to test,
Finding answers, never at rest.

Each blend a different tale to tell,
Mysteries hide in every swell.
Why do I drink? To ponder and muse,
In the depths of laughter, I will choose.

A cup of hope, rich and divine,
In bitter moments, sweetness aligns.
Life's answers brewed like a magic trick,
Stirred with humor, brewed to pick.

The grind of beans, the drip of fate,
In every filter, joy awaits.
So pass the mugs, let's share a toast,
To the roast that brings us the most!

Miles of Mindfulness

With every sip, I wander far,
Through thoughts and dreams, like a shooting star.
Coffee grounds spill like time in space,
I chase the laughter, the smiling face.

Roaming through bean fields, I align,
Sipping slowly, tasting the divine.
What's life's meaning? Oh, I'm not sure,
But with coffee's warmth, I feel secure.

On a journey with each warm pour,
Seeking joy in the mundane and more.
Moments caught in light and steam,
Life's a canvas, painted with dreams.

So raise your cup to the silly quest,
In every laugh, we find our rest.
With miles traveled, hand in hand,
Coffee's the compass, guiding our land.

The Flavorful Path to Insight

In the morning light we meet,
With a cup of joy, oh so sweet.
Philosophers once said, 'Take a sip',
I mutter, 'Life's a brew, don't let it drip!'

Beans are roasted, dreams take flight,
Mixing laughter, sugar, and delight.
Stirring thoughts with every gulp,
I smile and say, 'Hey, what's the hullabaloo?'

Chasing shadows while I stir,
Questions dance like cream in my burr.
Espresso shots, the truth unfolds,
With every sip, revelation molds.

So with each cup, I roam and play,
Seeking wisdom in the light of day.
Now who needs deep talks and lore?
Just hand me coffee, and I'll explore!

Chasing Shadows with a Latte

In the quiet café, I muse,
With a latte in hand, I won't lose.
Sipping foam like it's my fate,
Wondering how to translate.

With every swirl, a new thought flies,
Is it the drink or the caffeine high?
Philosophy within a cup,
I guess it's time to fill it up.

Nonsense hums between the sips,
Stories drip from eager lips.
The cosmic dance of milk and brew,
Funny how it all feels so true.

Chasing shadows, laughter roars,
Wisdom brews behind café doors.
With each new cup, a fresh delight,
Who knew the secrets brewed so bright?

Stirring Thoughts and Stirring Souls

A pot of dreams, a kettle's song,
Life's complexity feels so wrong.
But over coffee, it's not so bad,
Sip it slow, or you'll be mad.

Stirring thoughts within my brew,
Finding joy in the overdue.
A splash of cream, perhaps some spice,
Life's sweet moments come with ice.

Conversations swirling near and far,
Coffee grounds are my guiding star.
In every cup, silly debates,
Why oh why can't we all relate?

So here I sit, mug in hand,
Searching for meaning in this wondrous land.
With every gulp, laughter will roll,
Brewed delights stir both heart and soul.

Brewed Wisdom

Morning pours like a magic spell,
Coffee highs; oh, can't you tell?
With each drop, an epiphany glows,
Of life's great questions nobody knows.

Found on this road, a donut too,
Sidekick to the coffee, it's true.
Wisdom brews with every bite,
Philosophers chuckle, 'What's the insight?'

So let's sip deep, stir our souls,
In caffeinated warmth, history rolls.
With frothy mustaches and puns afield,
To laughter and joy, we have to yield.

In espresso shots, I'll chase the sun,
Life's grand puzzle—let's have some fun!
For in every sip, there's truth to be found,
Brewed wisdom awaits, let's gather 'round!

Decoding Dreams

A cat in a hat, what does it mean?
Is it coffee or chaos, or something unseen?
I sip on my brew, grasping for clues,
My dreams brew questions, my mind fills with blues.

A toast to the nights I wander and roam,
Chasing the thoughts that feel like home.
Were those tacos I had? Or just a mirage?
Some things need coffee, not a full barrage.

The wise owl spins tales in whimsical flight,
As I gulp down my java, it feels just so right.
Could meaning be hiding in frothy milk foam?
Should I buzz with caffeine or just call it home?

So here's to the dreams that tickle and tease,
With laughter and coffee, I aim to appease.
I'll stir and I'll ponder, but mostly I'll sip,
Join me in this madness, let's take a quick trip.

A Cup of Courage

With each slurp of warmth, I muster my might,
Facing the workday, oh what a fright!
But coffee's my sidekick, my panther of strength,
I'll tackle my to-do list, go to great lengths.

In office armors, we conquer and brawl,
With mugs raised high, we laugh through it all.
Who needs a cape when you've got a brew?
I feel like a hero; my heart feels brand new.

Let's brew up a potion that sparks joy within,
A splash of adventure in every warm pin.
From tricky emails to meetings in rooms,
Fueled by this nectar, we dance past our glooms.

So fill up your cup, let's toast to the day,
With courage brewed strong, we'll find our own way.
In laughter and sips, we'll conquer the strife,
With a dash of good humor, we'll brew up our life.

Dark Roast Reflections

Staring in my cup, a dark abyss so deep,
Are thoughts brewing secrets or just lack of sleep?
With every bold sip, I ponder life's game,
Is it brewed correctly, or am I to blame?

Philosophers say, think hard with a frown,
But I add some cream, and I turn that around.
With laughter and jokes, we ponder the grind,
Is it the beans or the milk that shapes how we find?

From mugs of confusion to cups of delight,
I stir in some laughs to lighten the night.
Reflecting on beans that fortify cheer,
My dark roast reveals the meaning, I fear!

So let's brew together, in thought and in jest,
In the foam of our doubts, we'll find our quest.
With laughter and coffee, our hearts start to soar,
Let's savor this mystery, who could ask for more?

Liquid Philosophies

In steamy elixirs, we splash through the haze,
Searching for wisdom in caffeine-drenched days.
Is life just a whirl of flavors and froth?
Should we sip with a grin, or simply go goth?

Each gulp is a chance to ponder the stars,
With sips full of humor, we dance through our scars.
Did Socrates sip teas, or was he too pure?
I'll blend in some laughter to spark the obscure.

So here I sit, mug held tight like a friend,
Awash in the warmth, on that I depend.
In the swirl of ideas from rich beans of thought,
Philosophies bubble, remind me of what's sought.

Astute reflections mingle with playful delight,
As we sip down our dreams, spirits take flight.
Life's winding path may be slippery and steep,
But with coffee in hand, it's a joy not to weep.

Caffeine and Contemplation

In the morning light, a cup in hand,
Philosophers gather, ready to stand.
Steaming thoughts swirl, like milk in brew,
Where's meaning hiding? Oh, where are you?

Sip by sip, we ponder our fate,
Between the sips, we debate, we wait.
With foamy mustaches and a gleam in our eyes,
Searching for wisdom in coffee lies.

A pot of inspiration, brewed fresh each day,
Stirring reflections in a whimsical way.
Why does the coffee have to be hot?
Is life just a blend of cream and a lot?

So we chuckle and sip, letting worries fade,
With laughter and caffeine, a joyful charade.
Each drop a reminder, so rich and absurd,
We may never solve it, but it's fun to be heard!

In the Wake of Dreams

In the quiet night, dreams dance and spin,
I wake with a jolt, let the day begin.
Coffee the fuel for thoughts that take flight,
Will I find wisdom before it gets light?

Cups piled high, like mountains of hope,
Dodging deep thoughts as I try to cope.
Each sip a spark, igniting my brain,
Searching for answers in the caffeine rain.

Waking at dawn, a sleepy parade,
In my caffeine kingdom, I'm king, unafraid.
Mysteries linger like creamer's swirl,
Life's quirks unfurl in a caffeinated whirl.

So cheers to the mug, my loyal friend,
Together we laugh while others pretend.
In the wake of dreams, with a knowing grin,
Life's meaning may be in the coffee within!

Brewed Awakening

A pot on the stove, it bubbles with cheer,
Each boil a reminder life's mystery is near.
With a laugh and a yawn, I pour out my soul,
Yet questions remain, spilling black as a coal.

Sipping and searching for pearls of delight,
In mugs full of warmth on a chilly night.
Do I drink for the buzz or the thoughts that it brings?
Is wisdom just foam or the joy that it sings?

Roasted reflections in each tiny sip,
Fleeting perceptions as time starts to slip.
The answer may hide in the depths of my cup,
But life seems much clearer when coffee's held up.

So I raise my mug high to the morning sun,
With frothy delights, let the pondering fun.
In a world that confuses, I find my own way,
Through laughter and coffee, I'll start a new day!

Questions Whirl Like Steam

Each morning I rise with a mug in my grasp,
Questions abound in a waking gasp.
What makes us tick? What makes us glow?
Is it caffeine magic, or just for the show?

Steam rises high, carrying thoughts to the sky,
Why do I ponder as the cup gurgles by?
With a chuckle, I sip, let my mind start to roam,
Is this where I find my caffeine-filled home?

Each drop an inquiry, each swirl a jest,
The secrets of life in a steaming quest.
The more that I drink, the less I achieve,
Or is it just comfort that I want to believe?

So I laugh at each question, I savor each brew,
With coffee companion, I'm never less true.
In the heart of the mug, we share a good laugh,
Life might not make sense, but at least I have half!

Grounded Aspirations

In the morning light, the mug does gleam,
A caffeinated cup, oh what a dream!
With every sip, I ponder and muse,
Should I chase my goals, or just take a snooze?

I put on my shoes, ready to chase,
But suddenly coffee's my favorite place.
I set out with purpose, or so I think,
Only to stop for another drink!

The world is vast, horizons wide,
Yet in this café, I'll gladly abide.
Goals may be waiting, but so is this brew,
Life's mysteries are easier to chew!

So raise your cups to aspirations bold,
With laughter and warmth they brighten the cold.
I may not find answers, but cheers to the style,
For happiness brews in each jolly mile!

Traversing Through Taste

I wandered the aisles of the café galore,
A menu so vast, I'm knocked to the floor!
Espresso, macchiato, lattes galore,
Each sip a quest, I just can't ignore!

In a world of flavors, my heart beats like drums,
What's the meaning of life? Who needs it? Here it comes!

With whipped cream atop and sprinkles for flair,
I lose all my worries, just breathe in the air!

Sipping on mocha, contemplating fate,
With marshmallows bouncing, it's hard to debate.
Do chocolate dreams hold the keys to the soul?
Or is it just sugar that makes me feel whole?

So here's to the cups that inspire and thrill,
With each perfect pour, we dream and we chill.
With flavors so rich, I can't help but believe,
Life's more like a dessert, just dare to conceive!

The Brew of Awareness

Awake with a jolt, my senses alive,
This brew in my hand feels like I can thrive.
The aroma wraps round like a warm, snug hug,
Each sip a reminder: I'm not just a mug!

I ponder the meaning in cups filled with steam,
Wondering if life is a grand coffee dream.
Do we seek for the truth in the darkest of roasts?
Or in the cream corner, where sweet pleasure boasts?

With each little gulp, a thought must arise,
Am I just a barista in life's grand surprise?
Pouring out visions, I may be lost,
But it's fine, just fetch another cup, at what cost?

So I sip and I savor this bitter-sweet ride,
In foam and in laughter, let's take it in stride.
For the brew of awareness stirs more than just beans,
It unwraps the joy in our flavorful routines!

Questions in the Crema

In the frothy swirl of my morning delight,
I ponder my purpose with each dizzy bite.
What's hidden in crema, so soft, so profound?
Do my questions dissolve as I sip all around?

Why do I wonder if life's just a game?
When chocolate and cream can make dull days tame?
A sprinkle of joy in my cup lifts my plight,
Who would believe that it's brewed out of sight?

I ask the barista my thoughts in a hush,
"What's the secret?" I lean in, I rush.
With a wink and a smile, he hands me a brew,
"Answers come slower; just savor the hue!"

So here in this moment, I sip with glee,
Embracing the questions, letting them be.
For life's tasty riddles can surely absolve,
In the depths of my cup, all mysteries evolve!

Seeking Clarity in Each Sip

In the morning light, I pour,
Dark nectar flows, I crave for more.
Each drop a thought, a little spark,
In the coffee cup, I find my arc.

Stirring dreams with every sip,
Time to ponder, let it rip.
Why do socks disappear so fast?
Maybe caffeine holds the key at last.

Caffeinated whims dance through the air,
In a mug, my chaos laid bare.
With each slurp, I consider the day,
What to wear? Who to dismay?

Oh, the laughter brewed, it's no surprise,
As I twirl my spoon and fantasize.
Life's a puzzle, some pieces amiss,
Yet all feels grand with a caffeinated kiss.

Steam Rising, Questions Forming

Steam floats high, my mind's a race,
In the café, I find my space.
What's the purpose of all this cheer?
And where's the milk? Waiter, I fear!

With a frothy crown, it all begins,
Stirring thoughts, as daily spins.
Can coffee beans unlock the truth?
Or is the answer just the proof?

Laughter bubbles in this cup,
Sip it slow, don't spill it up.
Why do people chase the grind?
Hey, I just want peace of mind!

A magical elixir in my hand,
Guiding me through this wild land.
With every gulp, the questions flow,
Is happiness in lattes, or just for show?

Heartfelt Brews

Barista's art, a swirling delight,
A heart formed in foam, a morning sight.
Is love just caffeine, in a mug so warm?
Or is it something that breaks the norm?

Each bitter sip, a tale retold,
As if life's wisdom can be bold.
When did I last dance in the rain?
Oh right, it was after coffee; what a gain!

Blending flavors, sweet and strong,
Is there a right or wrong in this song?
Happiness is brewing on a whim,
With each cup, I dive deep within.

So raise your mugs, cheers to us,
In this cozy nook, there's no need to fuss.
Life's absurdities make us laugh and sigh,
Just don't forget, I still want that pie!

Savoring the Journey

With every pour, the journey starts,
In this café, we tell our hearts.
What is purpose? A riddle to sip,
As I savor each bittersweet trip.

Wandering thoughts in a caffeinated haze,
Finding meaning in the oddest ways.
Like why do cats sit on your lap?
Is there truth in this cozy trap?

The aroma wafts, a fragrant guide,
As questions bubble up inside.
Who knew the answers were so near?
In a cup of joy and a splash of cheer.

So let's toast to life's funny bends,
With every brew, we make amends.
To the quirks we share and endless chats,
Where meaning brews—amongst the spats!

A Brewed Awakening

In the morning light, I rise with cheer,
A cup in hand, I have no fear.
The world awaits, so vast and wide,
But first, my friend, let's enjoy this ride.

Beans are ground, the water's hot,
A ritual that hits the spot.
Sip the nectar, feel it flow,
Wisdom blooms in caffeine's glow.

Chasing dreams with frothy foam,
Finding meaning, I call it home.
I ponder life's great mysteries,
While clutching my cup, just me and teas.

So here's to joy in every pour,
Each sip reveals a little more.
In laughter brewed with every cup,
I raise my mug—life's ups and downs!

Sips of Enlightenment

A latte here, a mocha there,
With every sip, I face my dare.
Spilling thoughts over cappuccino,
Finding peace like a pro casino.

Espresso shots, my holy grail,
In frothy realms, I set my sail.
Philosophy pours like heavy cream,
While I stir my thoughts—it's quite a dream.

Doughnuts by my side, a fitting team,
Together we weave a sugary theme.
Life's not a puzzle, it's more a brew,
With flavors mixed, what's old is new.

In every sip, a jest, a quip,
Each doughy bite—another trip.
Pour it strong, let the laughter flow,
With each sweet slug, I steal the show!

Paths Through the Grind

Awake but tired, I play my card,
Chasing dreams, though it's hard.
My compass swings with every sip,
Navigating life, a caffeine trip.

Filters drip, and so do thoughts,
Finding answers in what's sought.
A dash of cream, a sprinkle of fun,
Brewing wisdom till the day is done.

Fumbling through cups, a quest at hand,
In messy kitchens, we make our stand.
Staring deep in each warm embrace,
Searching for meaning in pumpkin spice grace.

So I laugh and sip, and spill a few,
Life's just a dance; I'll sip to it too.
With beans in my heart, I'll find the way,
Through the grind and laughter, I'll seize the day!

Cups of Clarity

In quirky cafes, ideas ignite,
With mugs in hand, we share our plight.
Chuckle at chaos, sip with glee,
Savoring moments, you and me.

The jitters come, the laughter peaks,
As coffee brews, it softly speaks.
Each sip unravels the tightest knots,
Shaking our heads at forgotten thoughts.

Hazelnut dreams and caramel flair,
Finding the truth in the steamy air.
Giggles blend with swirling steam,
Over brewed pools, we dare to dream.

So let's fill our cups once more,
With chitchat rich, we'll explore.
Life's a puzzle; we'll sip and divine,
With camaraderie steeped—our hearts entwine!

Epiphanies in the Steam

In a mug so brown, a truth does brew,
Wonders arise, when life feels askew.
Caffeine dreams dance in my sight,
As I ponder what's wrong and what's right.

Sips of wisdom, each drop a clue,
A splash of milk, redefining the view.
In the morning haze, I clutch my cup tight,
An escape from the chaos, a morning delight.

The world slows down in this coffee trance,
Pour over the moments, give joy a chance.
Between sips of laughter, I find my way,
Exploring life's quirks—come what may.

So here's to the brew that brings us cheer,
In the swirling steam, our thoughts appear.
A light-hearted quest for the bright unknown,
In a cup of joe, we find our own.

Coffee Chronicles

Every morning starts with a call,
A ritual of sorts, I mustn't stall.
I grind my beans, watch them swirl,
The magic begins, oh what a world!

With each dark drop, I feel alive,
Like a caffeine-fueled bee on a hive.
Philosophers sip, poets create,
With java in hand, life feels first-rate.

Adventures await in every pour,
A splash of cream opens new doors.
I scribble thoughts, the words flow fast,
Will this cup hold answers—the die is cast!

So cheers to the brews, the highs and lows,
In every mug, a story grows.
Laughing out loud, sipping away,
Together we brew and seize the day!

Stirring the Soul

With a spoon's gentle clink, I stir my fate,
A swirl of joy, it's never too late.
In steaming depths, I seek what's real,
As the warmth rises, I start to feel.

Oh the coffee grounds, they know so well,
Whispers of secrets they're eager to tell.
In every gulp, I taste the thrill,
Finding meaning in caffeine's sweet chill.

The clock ticks slow, while thoughts race by,
Each sip an answer to the curious why.
With chuckles and grins, I sip and sigh,
In the coffee's embrace, time seems to fly.

So let's raise our cups and join in the cheer,
For moments like these, bring us near.
To stir up the soul, to laugh and play,
In this caffeinated joy, we find our way!

Mindful Sips

In the morning light, with a cup in hand,
I pause and ponder, it's just so grand.
Warmth wraps around, like a cozy hug,
With each mindful sip, life starts to unplug.

The world rushes by, but I take my time,
Savoring flavors like a soft rhyme.
Through chocolate notes and caramel swirls,
I chuckle at life's silly little whirls.

Sipping by the window, I watch the parade,
While dreams in the steam happily invade.
A hint of laughter, a dash of cheer,
In my favorite mug, there's nothing to fear.

So lift that cup, let good vibes flow,
In these mindful sips, let the good times grow.
With joy in each taste and hearts that glow,
Let's stir up the magic that coffee can show!

Brewed Questions

What's the purpose of waking, my dear?
If the coffee pot's empty, it's clear.
Is it finding true love, or just cream?
Or the joys of a good caffeinated dream?

With each sip, I ponder the stars,
Are they there for our joy, or to jar?
Should I take life serious, or laugh?
Can I find it all at my local cafe?

Is it in striving or just sipping slow?
In the froth or the brew, I seek to know.
Pour me another and let's have a chat,
For existential musings, let's not fall flat!

When life gives you lemons, just add lattes,
With whipped cream on top, it all more play.
So I toast to the days, whatever they bring,
With coffee in hand, I venture in swing.

Whirlwinds of Flavor

In a whirlpool of beans, I commence,
Each swirl a thought, so intense.
With coffee swirling in my cup,
I wonder if I'm really just a pup.

What comes first, the brew or the grind?
In these riddles, I hope to find.
The meaning of life or who made the blend,
All solved when I pour, drink, and pretend.

With frothy fables in a mug,
Every flavor is a memory hug.
A sprinkle of laughter, a dash of time,
In this café world, I'm in my prime!

So let's tango with sugar and cream,
Dance with the dark roast and frothy dream.
For each sip teaches me more than before,
Even if it's just to come back for more.

Sipping Through Existence

Sipping my way through the daily grind,
Is there wisdom in caffeine? I might find.
With each cup, I dive deeper within,
To discover if life's just a spin.

Microchips or coffee beans, which am I?
In the hustle and bustle, do I fly?
A life in bubbles, or one freshly brewed,
Is existence just about being in mood?

From lattes to espressos, I make my toast,
Raising my cup to what I love most.
Let's muse on the essence, while we sip,
Each drop, a journey, a moment to grip.

With laughter and flavors swirling around,
In this café life, joy's always found.
So brew me a thought, let's explore the fun,
In coffee's warm glow, we are never done.

Musing Over Mocha

A dash of cocoa, a sprinkle of cheer,
Is this life's secret, or just my beer?
In every mocha, a riddle lies,
More intriguing than the bluest skies.

Sipping slowly, I chase my thoughts,
Am I a philosopher or just getting shots?
Each sweet drip leads me down new tracks,
Where the coffee's thick, there's no looking back!

Whispers of cinnamon linger and tease,
While pondering if I should take it with ease.
Is the answer in the foam or the brew?
Or perhaps it's just—ah! Another cuppa, woohoo!

So in this café of questions and whim,
Let's raise our mugs, let laughter brim.
For life's a blend, full of beans and delight,
Together we sip into the night.

Echoes in a Coffee Cup

In the morning light, I sip and sigh,
Wondering why my dreams run dry.
Caffeine whispers secrets from the brew,
Each drop a riddle, oh what to do?

A swirl of cream, a sprinkle of hope,
I search for wisdom, but can't quite cope.
Stirring my thoughts, like sugar in foam,
Is this cup of joe, my soul's true home?

With each little sip, I ponder it all,
What's life's great prize, the chocolate or the thrall?
The laughter of friends, the warmth of the mug,
I'll settle for joy, just give me a hug!

As caffeine kicks in, I dance with glee,
Finding connections, like stars, you see?
In this coffee realm, I find my way,
With each steaming cup, I'm ready to play!

Seeking Solace in Dark Roasts

Amidst the grind, I search for bliss,
In dark roasted depths, I find my kiss.
The earthy aroma, a warm embrace,
With every sip, I quicken my pace.

The world's a circus, and I'm the clown,
Pouring my heart, face up, not down.
Each gulp a giggle, each slurp a cheer,
Finding life's meaning with each coffee near.

Through froth and bubbles, my thoughts collide,
Pouring my troubles, becoming my guide.
A latte art heart, a mocha delight,
Finding my purpose in each sunny bite.

So I raise my cup, let the laughter flow,
In every dark roast, there's something to show.
When life gets murky, and times seem tough,
Just brew a strong batch, that's always enough!

Percolating Thoughts

Percolating dreams in a coffee pot,
Stirred by the grind, each thought a shot.
Bubbling ideas, they froth and swell,
Brewing a story, I've something to tell.

Beans burst with laughter, grounds hold the key,
To unlock the mysteries, come sit with me.
As steam rises high, so do my hopes,
With each merry sip, I learn how to cope.

I ponder life's questions, like sugar in cream,
Stirring my fate in a caffeinated dream.
With every hot cup, the answers come clear,
In the swirl of the brew, I lose all my fear.

So let's raise our mugs, let's toast the night,
To the trials and tribulations, to wrongs made right.
With caffeine as fuel, we take on the world,
In this zany adventure, our flags are unfurled!

Beyond the Beans: Journey to Self

Beyond the beans, I roam so wide,
With coffee as compass, it's my joyride.
Each mug's a portal, each cup a chance,
To find deeper meaning, to join the dance.

In cafés I ponder, in diners I dream,
While sipping on brews that bubble and steam.
A journey of laughter, a quest for the bold,
With caffeine as magic, new stories unfold.

Like pouring a blend on a Saturday morn,
I'm seeking the stories that life has worn.
I find joy in sips, in every new grind,
As I brew up a laugh, and leave woes behind.

In the depths of the cup, I ponder it all,
The joys and the mishaps, the rise and the fall.
I'll cherish the moments, let my heart leap,
In the realm of coffee, my soul's secrets keep!

www.ingramcontent.com/pod-product-compliance
Lightning Source LLC
Chambersburg PA
CBHW051654160426
43209CB00004B/888